Jesse Owens
The Fastest Man Alive

by Barbara A. Donovan
illustrated by Don Dyen

SCHOOL PUBLISHERS

Copyright © by Harcourt, Inc.

All rights reserved. No part of this publication may be reproduced or transmitted in any form or by any means, electronic or mechanical, including photocopy, recording, or any information storage and retrieval system, without permission in writing from the publisher.

Requests for permission to make copies of any part of the work should be addressed to School Permissions and Copyrights, Harcourt, Inc., 6277 Sea Harbor Drive, Orlando, Florida 32887-6777. Fax: 407-345-2418.

HARCOURT and the Harcourt Logo are trademarks of Harcourt, Inc., registered in the United States of America and/or other jurisdictions.

Printed in the United States of America

ISBN 10: 0-15-350304-1
ISBN 13: 978-0-15-350304-7

Ordering Options
ISBN 10: 0-15-349941-9 (Grade 6 ELL Collection)
ISBN 13: 978-0-15-349941-8 (Grade 6 ELL Collection)
ISBN 10: 0-15-357345-7 (package of 5)
ISBN 13: 978-0-15-357345-3 (package of 5)

If you have received these materials as examination copies free of charge, Harcourt School Publishers retains title to the materials and they may not be resold. Resale of examination copies is strictly prohibited and is illegal.

Possession of this publication in print format does not entitle users to convert this publication, or any portion of it, into electronic format.

2 3 4 5 6 7 8 9 10   179   12 11 10 09 08 07

From J.C. to Jesse

On September 12, 1913, Henry and Emma Owens welcomed their tenth child into the world. His name was James Cleveland Owens. He was called J.C. by his family and friends.

The Owens family lived in Oakville, Alabama. They were very poor. J.C.'s father worked on a farm that he didn't own. They barely had enough money for clothes.

Everyone had to help out on the farm. J.C. worked in the fields even as a young child. He planted and picked cotton.

Little J.C. was sick a lot. In the winter, he'd often get a terrible fever. J.C. also developed other health problems that his mother treated. The family could not afford to pay for a doctor.

Still, J.C. Owens had a happy childhood. He played baseball. He also fished in the pond and played tag. He liked running games the most. They made him feel happy and powerful. Later in life, he said, "I always loved running. I wasn't very good at it, but I loved it because it was something you could do all by yourself, and under your own power. You could go in any direction, fast or slow as you wanted, fighting the wind if you felt like it, seeking out new sights just on the strength of your feet and the courage of your lungs."

   When J.C. was about nine years old, he and his family left the farm in Alabama. They moved to Cleveland, Ohio. They hoped that J.C.'s father would find a job that paid well. J.C.'s father had little luck. As a result, everyone in the family took whatever jobs they could find. Even J.C. took jobs after school. He did things such as running errands and shining shoes.
   J.C. got the name *Jesse* at school in Cleveland. When he started school there, his teacher asked him his name. His teacher thought he said "Jesse Owens" when he really said "J.C. Owens." His teacher wrote his name in her record book as Jesse. That is what people called him from then on.

The Chance to Run

A few years later, when Jesse was in junior high school, he met a man who would change his life—Charles Riley. Mr. Riley was the physical education teacher at Jesse's school. He was also the coach of the school's track-and-field team. Mr. Riley knew that Jesse could be a star on his team.

Mr. Riley offered to work with Jesse after school. Jesse didn't know what to do. He had jobs after school each day. His family needed that money. Jesse wanted Mr. Riley's help, but he could not let his family down. Jesse told Mr. Riley about his jobs. Mr. Riley came up with a solution to the problem. He would help Jesse before school each day.

Jesse worked hard on his running. He practiced the exercises that Mr. Riley taught him. Jesse was eventually ready to compete. He ran in junior high track meets. Then in 1928, Jesse set his first world record. It was the junior high school world record for the high jump. Jesse jumped 6 feet (1.8 m) up and over the pole. Then he set a second world record. He jumped 22 feet 11.75 inches (7.0 m) in the long jump. He had become the best junior high school jumper in the world.

In high school, Jesse continued to do well in all his events. Jesse got ready for each competition with his coach's help. By the spring of 1932, Jesse had won so many events that he seemed like a one-person team.

　　Big Ten schools were universities with some of the best and toughest programs for athletes. Jesse decided to go to Ohio State University, a Big Ten university in his home state. He did not get any help from the university to pay for his education. Jesse pumped gas, ran an elevator, and did other jobs to pay for school. Working several jobs and studying didn't bother Jesse as long as he could do what he loved best—run.

　　In May of 1935, Jesse competed in the Big Ten Championship meet. In less than an hour, Jesse tied one world record and broke three other world records. He now held the world record for the 100-meter dash. He was the "fastest man alive." Jesse was ready to compete in the biggest competition of all—the Olympic Games.

Olympic Gold

In 1936, the Olympics were held in Berlin, Germany. The German leader at that time was Adolph Hitler. Hitler did not believe in treating all people equally, including African Americans. Hitler thought some people were better than others. When Jesse Owens arrived in Berlin for the games, he was no stranger to being treated unfairly. Often in his life, he'd been treated poorly because of the color of his skin. He would not let what Hitler thought affect him.

As always, Jesse put pressure on himself to win at the Olympics. He had trained hard. He did not want to lose. On August 3, he prepared for the final race in the 100-meter dash. In just 10.3 seconds, Jesse Owens reached the finish line. His victory in the race caused the people in the stands to cheer for him. On that day, people did not care about the color of his skin. They loved him because he was a great athlete. Jesse had won his first Olympic gold medal.

The next day, Jesse had to compete in the long jump. Jesse didn't do well on his first two jumps. If he failed on his third jump, he would not make it to the finals. Jesse ran as hard as he could, and his jump was long enough to get him into the finals. That afternoon, Jesse jumped 26 feet 5.25 inches (about 8 m). He won his second Olympic gold medal. He also set a new Olympic record for the long jump.

On the afternoon of August 5, Jesse was ready to run in the finals of the 200-meter dash. When the starting gun went off, Jesse sprang out onto the track. In 20.7 seconds, he was across the finish line. He had just broken another Olympic record. He had also won his third gold medal of the games.

Jesse had only planned to run in three events. However, his coach decided to have Jesse run on the 400-meter relay team. In a relay race, each runner on the team has to hand off a stick called a baton to the next runner. Jesse ran first. Jesse's team won the race in 39.8 seconds. They set a new Olympic record. They had also set a new world record. Jesse Owens, that poor, sickly boy from Oakville, Alabama, had just won his fourth Olympic gold medal. He was the best. Now the whole world knew it.

Scaffolded Language Development

REVIEW ORDINAL NUMBERS Review the selection with students, pointing out any ordinal numbers: <u>first</u> world record, <u>second</u> Olympic gold medal, <u>third</u> gold medal and <u>fourth</u> gold medal. Remind students that many ordinal numbers are formed by simply adding the letters *th* to the end of the number. Review the list of irregular ordinals and suggest that students simply need to memorize these.

first	second
third	fifth
eighth	ninth
twelfth	twentieth

Have students practice ordinal numbers by sitting in a circle and counting off around the circle by ordinal numbers from first to twentieth.

🌐 Social Studies

Olympics History Since 1896, the Olympic Games have been cancelled several times due to world events. Have students find out which Olympic Games were cancelled and why. Have them write several sentences about each cancelled event.

School-Home Connection

Sports Heroes Have students discuss their favorite sports heroes with family members. Then have them make a list of the qualities these athletes have shown that make them worthy of admiration. Suggest that students keep those qualities in mind as they try to achieve their own goals.

Word Count: 1,152